THE
GRILLED CHEESE
COOKBOOK

BECKS WILKINSON

Photography by Tom Regester

K

An Hachette UK Company
www.hachette.co.uk

First published in Great Britain in 2023 by Kyle Books,
an imprint of Octopus Publishing Group Ltd
Carmelite House, 50 Victoria Embankment,
London EC4Y 0DZ
www.octopusbooks.co.uk

Distributed in the US by
Hachette Book Group
1290 Avenue of the Americas, 4th and 5th Floor,
New York, NY 10104

Distributed in Canada by
Canadian Mando Group
664 Annette St, Toronto, Ontario, Canada, M65 2C8

ISBN 978-1-8041-9110-1

A CIP catalogue record for this book is
available from the British Library

Printed and bound in China

10 9 8 7 6 5 4 3 2

Publisher: Lucy Pessell
Designer: Isobel Platt
Editor: Feyi Oyesanya
Assistant Editor: Samina Rahman
Production Controller: Serena Savini

*This material was previously published
as Melt It.*

CONTENTS

THE GRILLED CHEESE SANDWICH

Everyone loves a sandwich – who doesn't? – but when you smother said sandwich in cheese and melt it, well, that just takes it to the next level: sandwich heaven.

I can honestly say I've never met anyone who doesn't enjoy a good toastie, kids and adults alike. They are the ultimate comfort food, and they can answer your cravings at any time of day – breakfast, lunch, midnight snack... Grilled cheese sandwiches (or toasties for the Brits) are quick, cheap and most of all, easy to make. With minimum effort you can turn the humblest of ingredients into a mouthwateringly decadent, towering sandwich or a much-needed hangover cure. So let's get melting!

THE EQUIPMENT

I've tried to keep this as simple as possible, which is why we will be skipping the toasted sandwich machine and making use of a trusty frying pan instead. I'm sure we all have fond childhood memories of using our toasted sandwich machines, and by all means, feel free to try some of these recipes out in yours if you have one, but they tend to limit you a certain size and type of bread. We don't want limits when it comes to our cheese toasties, plus everyone has a frying pan, right? So there will be no stopping you – just make sure it's big enough to hold the sandwich...

• **Non-stick frying pan** – non-stick is definitely best, or the melted cheese will stick like crazy and you can end up with a sticky mess

• **Cast-iron griddle pan** – for those all-important fancy bar marks when you're trying to impress your date with your top-notch sandwich

• **Spatula or fish slice** – for flipping your sandwich

• **Bread knife** – for slicing, of course

• **Bowl** – for prepping your all-important additions

• **Greaseproof paper**

That should just about cover it – although you may end up needing an oven if you decide to concoct such a Mega Tower of Cheesy Goodness that it won't melt in a pan...

This book is about making the best cheese toasties known to man and woman.
So it's important to start with the best quality ingredients you can find.

THE BREAD

You can't go wrong with good-quality sourdough bread.
It isn't too expensive – and, let's face it, most of your hipster
mates have probably grown beards and have their own
artisan sourdough starter bubbling away in the cupboard,
so beg a slice or two of the finished loaf from them.

I generally find day-old sourdough is better for toasting
as it doesn't crumble and gives a great texture. As a general
rule, aim for slices of about 2cm (¾ in) thick.

Depending on the sandwich, here are some other types
of bread and sweet treats you may want to try:

• Wholemeal or granary sourdough adds a nice nuttiness

• Rye bread

• Ciabatta

• Sliced white bloomer or sandwich loaf

• Brioche – for dessert sandwiches

• Panettone – a sweet fruity bread

• Bagels

• Doughnuts

• Waffles

WHOLEMEAL

RYE BREAD

BRIOCHE

THE CHEESE

When choosing cheese, you should always consider one vital factor:

MELTABILITY

There is nothing worse than chalky cheese in a hot sandwich – you want that oozy, melty, stringy, gooey deliciousness that crisps up at the edges and leaves you wanting more. I have made the enormous sacrifice of experimenting with mounds and mounds of the glorious stuff (I know, what a hero) in order to create the list below. These cheeses are all high in the meltability stakes, with excellent flavour and texture. The list could go on and on...feel free to go wild with your own experiments – after all that is how the best recipes come about.

- **Cheddar** – a classic when it comes to cheese toasties. Everyone has their own favourite, but I recommend Westcombe or Lincolnshire Poacher

- **Monterey Jack** – an American semi-hard cheese

- **Ogleshield** – a semi-hard cheese similar to Raclette, it melts beautifully

- **Mascarpone** – a mild, creamy cheese perfect in dessert sandwiches

- **Ricotta** – a very soft, slightly sweet cheese – another good choice for desserts

- **Goats' cheese** – a distinctive flavour that will really take your sandwiches to the next level

- **Gruyère** – a slightly sweet, salty hard cheese, it has a distinctive but not overpowering taste

- **Red Leicester** – similar to Cheddar, except it is slightly more crumbly and has an orangey red colour

- **Stilton** – a classic blue cheese with a strong flavour

YOU DON'T WANT A RED-HOT PAN – GENERALLY, AIM FOR A LOW TO MEDIUM HEAT SO YOUR SANDWICH WILL CRISP UP SLOWLY AND THE CHEESE WILL MELT, RATHER THAN BURNING ON THE OUTSIDE AND BEING COLD INSIDE.

ALWAYS, ALWAYS, EAT IMMEDIATELY! THIS IS OF THE HIGHEST PRIORITY.

BASIC INGREDIENTS

We have gone for variety and excitement in this book, so the ingredients do vary, but here are a few essentials that you should always have to hand to rustle up a top-quality toastie in a hurry.

• **Butter** – always butter, not margarine. Keep at room temperature for spreadability

• **Olive oil**

• **Mayonnaise**

• **Gherkins/pickles**

CONDIMENTS

CARAMELIZED ONION MARMALADE

This delicious sweet onion jam is perfect for The Classic sandwich on page 12.

MAKES 1 SMALL JAR

3 tablespoons olive oil
3 red onions, halved and sliced as thinly as possible
½ teaspoon salt
4 sprigs of thyme
2 tablespoons red wine vinegar
1 tablespoon soft brown sugar

Place a frying pan over a medium heat and add the oil. Once it's hot, add the onions and fry for 10 minutes. Add the salt and thyme sprigs, decrease the heat, then continue cooking for 10–15 minutes until the onions are a nice caramelized colour and all the liquid has evaporated.

Push the onions to one side of the pan and add the vinegar and sugar to the other side. Cook until dissolved, then stir it all together and keep cooking until you have a gorgeous sticky jam.

Transfer to a sterilzised jar. It will keep in the fridge for about 2 weeks.

SMOKY TOMATO KETCHUP

Of course you can just use shop-bought ketchup if you'd rather, but this homemade version adds a little smoke and spice. It's great with The Best in the Tuna-verse tuna melt (page 34), The Hangover (page 26) and anywhere else a little sauciness is required.

MAKES 1 SMALL JAR

1 teaspoon paprika
½ teaspoon coriander (cilantro) seeds
½ ground cloves
½ teaspoon garlic salt
8 plum tomatoes, roughly chopped
10 baby plum tomatoes on the vine, roughly chopped
1 red chilli, roughly chopped
2 red onions, roughly chopped
3 garlic cloves, roughly chopped
50ml (¼ cup) olive oil
200ml (1 cup) white wine vinegar
45g (¼ cup) soft brown sugar
salt and freshly ground black pepper

Preheat the oven to 180°C/gas mark 4.

Place a frying pan over a low–medium heat and add the paprika, coriander (cilantro) seeds and cloves. Toast until fragrant, then remove from the heat and transfer to a pestle and mortar along with the garlic salt. Grind to a powder.

Place the tomatoes, chilli, onions and garlic in a roasting tray. Drizzle with olive oil and sprinkle with salt, pepper and the ground spices. Cover the tray tightly in tin foil and transfer to the oven. Roast for 15–20 minutes.

Meanwhile, place the vinegar and sugar in a large saucepan over a medium heat. Cook until the sugar has dissolved. Once the tomatoes, onions and chilli have finished roasting, add them to this mixture and cook for a further 40 minutes.

Place the mixture in a blender and blitz until smooth. Transfer the finished ketchup to a sterilized jar until ready to use. It will keep in the fridge for about 2 weeks.

CARAMELIZED ONION MARMALADE

SMOKY TOMATO KETCHUP

QUICK-PICKLED ONIONS (PAGE 34)

PICKLED CUCUMBER (PAGE 25)

CHAPTER ONE

MARVELLOUS MELTS FOR EVERYDAY

SIMPLE IDEAS AND SEXED-UP VERSIONS OF CLASSIC GRILLED CHEESE

THE CLASSIC
(CARAMELIZED ONION, THYME & CHEDDAR)

Cheddar and caramelized onion are a classic combo and the thyme kicks the whole thing up a notch, turning this into a melty masterpiece. If you don't have the time or inclination to make your own onion marmalade, you can always grab a jar from the shop.

2 tablespoons softened butter
4 slices of sourdough, 2cm (¾ in) thick
6 sprigs of thyme
4 tablespoons onion marmalade
(see page 8)

100g (4 oz) strong, mature Cheddar
(such as Westcombe), grated
salt and freshly ground black pepper

——— SERVES 2 ———

1. Place a non-stick frying pan over a medium heat.

2. Spread the butter over the sourdough slices and press a sprig of thyme into each piece. These will be the outsides of the toasties.

3. Turn over two of the slices and divide the onion marmalade evenly between them. Top the marmalade with the cheese, pressing it down.

4. Pick the leaves from the remaining thyme sprigs and sprinkle them over.

Season generously with salt and pepper. Top each with the other slices of bread, making sure the buttered side is on the outside.

5. Place the sandwiches into the pan and gently press down with a spatula.

6. Cook for about 4 minutes on each side until the cheese has melted and the bread is golden brown. Serve immediately with any remaining onion marmalade.

THE SECRET WEAPON
(CHEDDAR & HOT GREEN CHILLI SALSA)

This may look like an average grilled cheese sandwich, but hidden inside is a super spicy green chilli salsa that will blow your socks off.

4 slices of sourdough, 2cm (¾ in) thick
2 tablespoons butter
150g (5 oz) mature Cheddar, grated
salt and freshly ground black pepper

FOR THE CHILLI SALSA (MAKES 1 SMALL JAR)

½ teaspoon cumin
½ teaspoon coriander (cilantro) seeds
4 black peppercorns
zest and juice of 1 lime

1 green apple, ½ finely diced and ½ sliced
½ green (bell) pepper, finely diced
2 green chillies (or to taste), finely diced
½ red onion, finely diced
2 green bird's eye chillies, finely diced
1 tablespoon chopped coriander
  (cilantro) leaves
3 tablespoons olive oil
salt

— SERVES 2 —

1. Begin by making the green chilli salsa. In a dry frying pan over a medium heat, toast the cumin, coriander (cilantro) seeds and peppercorns for a few minutes until fragrant. Transfer to a pestle and mortar and grind to a fine dust.

2. Squeeze the lime juice over the diced apple to stop it oxidizing. Add to a bowl with the ground spices and all the other ingredients and mix well. Season with salt.

3. Place a non-stick frying pan over a medium heat.

4. Spread the butter over the sourdough slices. Turn over two of the slices and divide the sliced apple between them, then top with the grated Cheddar. Add 2 tablespoons of salsa to each one, then top with the other slices of bread, making sure the buttered side is on the outside.

5. Place the sandwiches into the pan and gently press down with a spatula. Cook for about 4 minutes on each side until the cheese has melted and the bread is golden brown. Serve immediately, with more salsa on the side. Any leftover salsa will keep in the fridge for 1 week.

THE WELSH RAREBIT
(OR SHOULD IT BE RABBIT...?)

**This is my tribute to one of the best-known melted cheese dishes.
No rabbits included!**

3 tablespoons butter
1 leek, finely sliced
1 tablespoon plain flour
1 teaspoon mustard powder
½ teaspoon paprika
200ml (1 cup) Guinness or other stout
250g (1 lb) Cheddar, grated

250g (1 lb) Lincolnshire Poacher, grated
(if you can't get it, just double the
amount of Cheddar instead)
dash Worcestershire sauce or
Tabasco
4 slices of sourdough, 2cm (¾ in) thick
1 spring onion (scallion), finely sliced

SERVES 4

1. Place a saucepan over a low heat. Add 1 tablespoon of the butter and, once it has melted, add the leek. Cook for 5 minutes until softened. Remove 2 tablespoons of the leeks and set aside for later. Add the flour, mustard powder and paprika to the remaining leeks and cook for 1 minute. Next, add the stout to the pan, stirring all the time as the mixture starts to thicken.

2. Add three-quarters of the cheese, along with a good dash of Worcestershire sauce or Tabasco. Continue to cook slowly until the cheese has melted.

3. Pour the mixture into a baking tray. Let it cool slightly, then transfer to the fridge to set for about 20 minutes. When it's ready, it should be thick enough to spoon.

4. Meanwhile, butter the bread.

5. Preheat the grill (broiler) to high. Divide the cheese mixture between all four slices of bread, then pop under the grill (broil) for 3–5 minutes until bubbly and golden. Top with the leeks and spring onion (scallion) and serve.

FOR A TOASTIE VERSION, JUST SANDWICH THE SLICES TOGETHER, BUTTER THE OUTSIDES OF THE BREAD AND FINISH IN THE FRYING PAN INSTEAD OF UNDER THE GRILL.

THE ITALIAN JOB
(ROASTED RED PEPPER, BRESAOLA & MOZZARELLA)

When it comes to melted cheese, mozzarella has to be one of the best – it's so satisfyingly melty and stringy. This sandwich celebrates some of the best Italian ingredients. The open texture of the ciabatta bread helps to create lovely pockets of pesto and cheese in every mouthful. For a quick version, use shop-bought roasted (bell) peppers and pesto instead.

1 red (bell) pepper, seeds and stalk
   removed, cut into quarters
1 tablespoon olive oil
1 ciabatta loaf
2 tablespoons butter
1 tablespoon finely grated Parmesan
125g (4 ½ oz) mozzarella
4 slices Bresaola
4 basil leaves
2 tomatoes, sliced

FOR THE PESTO
(OR YOU CAN USE SHOP-BOUGHT, IF YOU PREFER)
75g (¼ cup) Parmesan
10g (1 tbsp) pine nuts
30g (¼ cup) cashews
1 bunch basil, picked
1 garlic clove
150ml (1 cup) olive oil
juice of 1 lemon

— SERVES 2 —

1. Preheat the oven to 180°C/350°F/ gas mark 4. Place the (bell) pepper quarters on a roasting tray and drizzle with oil. Place in the oven to roast for ten minutes, then set aside.

2. Meanwhile, make the pesto. Heat a dry frying pan over a low heat. Add the pine nuts and cashews and gently toast for 3 minutes until golden brown. Set aside to cool.

3. Add the Parmesan to the blender, along with the toasted pine nuts and cashews, basil and garlic. Pulse until it forms a paste. Add the olive oil and the lemon juice and pulse again until you have your desired consistency.

4. Slice the ciabatta in half lengthways and butter the outside. Sprinkle the 1 tablespoon Parmesan over the buttered sides so that it sticks.

BELLISSIMO!

5. Turn the ciabatta over and spread the insides with 2 tablespoons of the pesto. Layer on the mozzarella, Bresaola, roasted (bell) peppers, tomatoes and basil leaves. Press the sandwich together.

6. Place the frying pan over a medium heat and lift the sandwich into it. Cook for 5 minutes on each side,

pressing it down with a spatula so that the Parmesan cheese on the outside crisps up. When the sandwich is golden brown and the mozzarella has melted, cut in two and serve immediately.

7. Any leftover pesto will keep in a jar in the fridge for up to 1 week.

THE SPANISH SENSATION
(MANCHEGO, MEMBRILLO, CHORIZO & ROCKET)

This is surprisingly easy, but make sure you don't let whoever you're cooking it for know that. The classic Spanish flavours make a great combination, but the real trick here is frying the chorizo first. This will release beautifully flavoured and fragrant oils into the pan. When you later add your sourdough, the bread will soak these oils up and take on all that glorious flavour. *¡Muy bien!*

100g (3 ½ oz) chorizo picante,
   thickly sliced
4 slices of sourdough, 2cm (¾ inch) thick
2 tablespoons membrillo (quince paste)
100g (4 oz) Manchego cheese, sliced

2 handfuls rocket (arugula) leaves
pinch of dried chilli flakes
1 tablespoon softened butter
freshly ground black pepper

SERVES 2

1. Place a non-stick frying pan over a medium heat. Once it has warmed up, add the chorizo and pan fry it for 5 minutes until it is crispy and releasing its aromatic oils. Transfer the chorizo to a plate, leaving the excess oil in the pan.

2. Lay out two slices of the sourdough bread and divide the quince paste between them, spreading it out evenly. Lay the sliced Manchego on top, then the fried chorizo. Finish each with a handful of rocket (arugula), and season with the chilli flakes and freshly ground black pepper before topping with the other slices of bread.

3. Butter the outsides of the sandwiches and return the pan to the heat. Place the sandwiches in the pan, slightly pressing down. The bread will soak up the chorizo oil and start to go golden and crispy. After 2–3 minutes, carefully flip over and brown the other side for 2–3 minutes until golden and melting. Eat immediately.

THE BRIE-L DEAL
(BRIE, CHARRED PEAR, CRANBERRY & SALAD LEAVES)

With rich, creamy brie, sweet pear caramelized on the griddle and the tang of cranberry, this is a rather grown up toastie. An excellent time to break out the granary bread. I recommend you use a cast-iron griddle pan for this one, to get seriously sexy bar marks.

2 pears, as firm as you can get, cored
    and sliced into wedges
2 tablespoons softened butter
4 slices of granary sourdough,
    2cm (¾ in) thick

2 tablespoons cranberry compote
100g (4 oz) brie, sliced
handful of salad leaves

—— SERVES 2 ——

1. Place a cast iron griddle pan over a medium–high heat. Let it get nice and hot.

2. Place the pear slices gently on the griddle and don't move them until you see them blacken and caramelize.

3. Meanwhile, spread the butter over the sourdough slices. Then turn over and spread the cranberry over two of the slices, on the unbuttered side. Top with the brie and charred pear slices, and cover each with salad leaves. Top with the other two slices of bread (butter side up) and lift into the griddle. Cook for 3–4 minutes, pressing down to get bar marks.

4. Once the bread is golden and the cheese is starting to melt, carefully flip to cook on the other side for 3–4 minutes.

5. Eat immediately.

Say cheese!

IF YOU CAN'T FIND
MONTEREY JACK, TRY
USING GOUDA INSTEAD.

THE SOZZLED SANDWICH
(KIMCHI, CHEDDAR & MONTEREY JACK)

This is what I like to call drunken cheese on toast. It's exactly what you need as a post-night out treat. Just make sure you don't leave the stove on...

2 tablespoons mayonnaise
1 tablespoon gochujang
4 slices of sourdough
2 tablespoons butter
75g (2 ½ oz) kimchi
75g (2 ½ oz) Cheddar, grated
75g (2 ½ oz) Monterey Jack, grated

FOR THE PICKLED CUCUMBER

1 small cucumber
2 tablespoons salt
1 red and 1 yellow chilli, halved
1 tablespoon picked dill
1 teaspoon coriander (cilantro) seeds
3 black peppercorns
200ml (1 cup) white wine vinegar
4 tablespoons caster (fine) sugar
2 garlic cloves, peeled and bruised

SERVES 2

1. Begin by making the pickled cucumber. Slice the cucumber in half lengthways and scrape out the seeds. Now sprinkle the salt over the cucumber. Leave for 30 minutes, then pour off any liquid from the cucumber and transfer to a bowl.

2. Place a small saucepan over a medium heat and add the remaining pickle ingredients, along with 100ml (½ cup) water. When the sugar has dissolved, remove from the heat and pour over the cucumber slices. Leave to cool.

3. Mix together the mayonnaise and gochujang. Place a non-stick frying pan over a medium heat to warm up.

4. Butter the bread, then turn two of the slices over. Spread with the gochujang mayo and divide the kimchi between them. Sprinkle a few of the pickled cucumber slices over the kimchi, then top with the cheeses. Top with the other two slices of bread, butter-side up. Transfer the sandwiches to the frying pan and cook for 3–4 minutes on each side until they are golden brown and the cheese has melted. Serve with the remaining pickled cucumber.

THE HANGOVER
(A FULL ENGLISH BREAKFAST IN A SANDWICH)

When you've overindulged the night before (maybe you even had a Sozzled Sandwich, see page 25), sometimes only a full English breakfast can save you. But once you've tried putting that breakfast between two slices of bread and adding a generous smothering of cheese, you'll never look back.

3 tablespoons olive oil

3 Cumberland sausages

4 rashers smoked back bacon

400g (14 oz) can baked beans

2 tablespoons harissa

100g (4 oz) mixed tomatoes, halved or whole

6 portobello mushrooms, sliced

a sprig of thyme, leaves only

a sprig of oregano, leaves only

4 slices of sourdough, 2cm (¾ inch) thick

2 tablespoons softened butter

100g (4 oz) Gouda, grated

2 eggs

smoky tomato ketchup (see page 8), to serve

salt and freshly ground black pepper

SERVES 2

1. Place a non-stick frying pan over a medium heat and add the oil. Once it has heated through, add the sausages and bacon and fry for about 10 minutes, turning occasionally, until cooked through and crispy. Remove from the pan and drain on a piece of kitchen towel. Cut the sausages in half lengthways.

2. Place a small saucepan over a low heat and add the baked beans to warm through. Stir in the harissa.

3. Meanwhile, add the tomatoes and mushrooms to the frying pan and fry for 4–6 minutes until golden. Sprinkle with the thyme and oregano, and season with salt and pepper. Remove from the pan and set aside.

4. Now it's time for the build. Preheat the grill (broiler) to medium. Grill (broil) the bread on one side, then flip over and butter it. Sprinkle the cheese over each slice, then return to the grill (broiler) for a few minutes to melt the cheese.

JUST WHAT THE
DOCTOR ORDERED

5. Place two of the cheese-on-toast slices on a plate, cheese side up. Divide the bacon and sausages between them, followed by the tomatoes and mushrooms.

6. Crack the eggs into the frying pan and cook for 5 minutes until the yolk is starting to set. Transfer the eggs on to the sandwiches and very carefully lift the sandwiches into the pan. Once the eggs are cooked to your liking, top the sandwiches with the other pieces of cheesy toast.

7. Serve with the spicy baked beans and lashings of ketchup.

THE CROQUE MADAME
(FRENCH-STYLE SANDWICH TOPPED WITH AN EGG)

A favourite in Parisian cafés since the early 1900s.

2 tablespoons softened butter
4 slices of sourdough, 2cm (¾ in) thick
8 sage leaves
1 tablespoon Dijon mustard
4 slices good-quality ham
100g (4 oz) Gruyère, grated
100g (4 oz) Monterey Jack, grated
1 tablespoon olive oil
2 eggs

FOR THE BÉCHAMEL SAUCE
350ml (1 ½ cups) milk
a grating of nutmeg
2 tablespoons butter
4 tablespoons plain flour
salt and freshly ground black pepper

SERVES 2

1. To make the béchamel, place the milk and nutmeg in a pan over a low heat and gently warm through. In a separate pan, melt the butter over a medium heat. Add the flour and mix into a paste. Slowly add the warmed milk, whisking, until the mixture has thickened and there are no lumps. Season and set aside.

2. Preheat the grill (broiler) to medium or the oven to 180°C/350°F/gas mark 4. Butter the bread and stick two sage leaves to each slice. Turn two slices over and, on the other side, spread the mustard. Top this with 1 tablespoon of béchamel for each slice, then 2 pieces of ham. Sprinkle with grated cheese and top with the other slices of bread, butter side out.

3. Place an ovenproof non-stick frying pan over a medium heat and, once it is hot, carefully add the sandwiches. Cook for 3–4 minutes, then flip and cook on the other side. Spread the remaining béchamel on top and place under the grill (broiler) or in the oven until golden.

4. Meanwhile, heat 1 tablespoon oil in a separate pan. Add the eggs and fry to your liking. When cooked, lift out and place on top of the bubbling béchamel. Eat immediately.

THE GREEK
(CHICKEN, FETA, OLIVES & TZATZIKI)

A towering tribute to the best of Greek ingredients.

2 tablespoons softened butter
4 slices of sourdough, 2cm (¾ in) thick
2 heritage tomatoes, sliced
½ red onion, finely sliced
1 tablespoon fresh oregano
8 kalamata olives
½ cucumber, halved and deseeded
100g (4 oz) cooked chicken breast, shredded
125g (4 ½ oz) mozzarella, sliced
75g (2 ½ oz) feta, crumbled
freshly ground black pepper

FOR THE TZATZIKI

100g (½ cup) Greek yogurt
2 tablespoons chopped mint leaves
1 garlic clove, grated
juice and zest of ½ lemon
½ teaspoon dried mint
1 tablespoon olive oil
salt and freshly ground black pepper

— SERVES 2 —

1. Preheat the oven to 180°C/350°F/gas mark 4.

2. Combine all the tzatziki ingredients in a bowl. Season to taste and set aside.

3. Butter the bread and then turn two of the slices over. Layer the tomatoes on these slices, followed by the red onion. Sprinkle with oregano and black pepper and then top with the olives. Slice the cucumber and lay on top. Mix the shredded chicken with 3 tablespoons of the tzatziki and divide this mixture between the two slices.

4. Place the cheeses on top of the tower, then finish with the remaining slices of bread. Place an ovenproof non-stick frying pan over a medium–high heat. Carefully place the sandwiches in the pan and cook for 3–4 minutes until starting to brown. Very carefully flip over and transfer to the oven until the cheese has melted. Serve with remaining tzatziki.

THE B.A.T. (AND C.)

The B.L.T. is an age-old classic, but swapping the lettuce for avocado avoids limp leaves, and adding a hefty helping of rich, creamy fontina cheese gives it a whole new lease of life. This sandwich is generously stuffed, so it can be a bit of a handful – but that's why we love it.

1 tablespoon olive oil
8 rashers (sliced) smoked back bacon
2 tablespoons softened butter
4 slices of sourdough, 2cm (¾ in) thick
2 tablespoons mayonnaise

100g (4 oz) fontina, grated
6 heritage tomatoes, sliced
1 avocado, peeled, stoned and sliced
salt and freshly ground pepper

SERVES 2

1. Place a non-stick frying pan over a medium-high heat. Once it's hot, add the oil, heat, and then add the bacon. Fry the rashers for a few minutes on each side until crisp. Transfer the bacon to a plate lined with kitchen towel to drain and set aside.

2. Butter all four slices of bread, then turn over and spread mayonnaise over the other sides. Divide the cheese between the four slices, on top of the mayo.

3. Now layer the tomatoes on two of the slices of bread, followed by the avocado. Top with the bacon, season with salt and pepper and finish with the other slices of bread, cheese-and-mayo side down and butter side up.

4. Return the frying pan to the heat and carefully lift the sandwiches into the pan. They will be quite full, so take care! Cook for 3–5 minutes until golden and the cheese is melting.

5. Eat immediately.

THE PROTEIN BOOST
(SPINACH, MUSHROOM & CHEESE OMELETTE GRILLED SANDWICH)

This is a gloriously melty mash-up of a cheese toastie and an omelette.
It makes a brilliant brunch and, with the spinach, mushrooms and tomatoes,
even manages to feel a bit good for you.

FOR THE OMELETTE

1 tablespoon butter
3 eggs
50g (1 ¾ oz) mixed mushrooms, sliced
1 tablespoon chopped flat-leaf parsley
100g (4 oz) Gruyère cheese, grated
salt and freshly ground black pepper

FOR THE BUILD

1 small baguette, halved lengthways
1 tablespoon softened butter
handful baby spinach
4 heritage tomatoes, sliced
1 red chilli, sliced

SERVES 2

---

1. Preheat the oven to 180°C/350°F/ gas mark 4.

2. Crack the eggs into a bowl, season with salt and pepper and whisk.

3. Butter the baguette inside and out and layer on the tomatoes, the chilli and about half of the spinach leaves. Set aside.

4. Heat a non-stick frying pan over a medium heat and add 1 tablespoon butter until foaming. Add the mushrooms and fry until browned.

    Pour in the eggs and slowly mix in the remaining spinach and the parsley. Sprinkle over about two thirds of the cheese.

5. Once the omelette has started to set, fold it in half and carefully place it in the baguette. Sprinkle the remaining cheese on top and transfer to a baking tray. Place it in the oven for 5 minutes until the cheese has melted. Eat immediately.

HEALTHY SPINACH

THE BEST IN THE TUNA-VERSE
(A POSH TUNA MELT WITH QUICK-PICKLED ONIONS)

This is a rather fancy version of the humble tuna melt, jazzed
up with delicious quick-pickled red onion and paprika.
It's pretty much out of this world.

160g (5 oz) can tuna (the posher,
   the better)
2 tablespoons mayonnaise
½ teaspoon paprika
1 spring onion (scallion), sliced
2 tablespoons softened butter
4 slices of granary sourdough,
   2cm (¾ in) thick
150g (5 ½ oz) raclette
smoky tomato ketchup (see page 8),
   to serve

FOR THE QUICK-PICKLED ONIONS

1 red onion, thinly sliced into rounds
juice of 1 lemon
½ teaspoon salt
½ teaspoon sugar

——— SERVES 2 ———

1. Start by making the quick-pickled
   onions. Place the red onion slices in
   a bowl and squeeze over the lemon
   juice. Add the salt and sugar, stir
   and set aside. The onions will soften
   and go bright pink in colour.

2. Drain the tuna and place in a
   bowl with the mayonnaise,
   paprika and spring onion (scallion).
   Stir to combine.

3. Place a non-stick frying pan over a
   medium heat to warm up.

4. Butter the bread, then turn two of
   the slices over so they are butter-
   side down. Spread the tuna-mayo
   mixture on these slices of bread,
   followed by a scattering of the
   quick-pickled onions and the
   cheese. Top with the other slices of
   bread, butter-side up.

5. Lift the sandwiches into the pan and
   cook for 3–5 minutes on each side
   until golden brown and the cheese
   is melted. Serve with the remaining
   onions and smoky tomato ketchup.

QUICK PICKLED
ONIONS... VERY PINK!

CUBAN-STYLE MEDIANOCHE
(ROAST PORK, PICKLES, HOT MUSTARD & SWISS CHEESE)

Medianoche translates as midnight. This sandwich is so named because it's a popular late-night snack in Havana's clubs. It's traditionally made with an egg-based bread – something like challah or brioche will work just fine. You will need something weighty like a pestle and mortar to press down on the sandwich – essential for a good medianoche. Although it would be perfect for a midnight feast, don't limit yourself – enjoy this melty delight any time, day or night.

2 tablespoons softened butter
4 slices of challah or brioche
1 tablespoon mayonnaise
100g (3 ½ oz) roast pork, sliced
100g (3 ½ oz) wafer thin ham

1 red chilli, sliced
4 gherkins (pickles)
100g (4 oz) Swiss cheese
1 tablespoon hot mustard

—— SERVES 2 ——

1. Place a griddle pan over a medium heat to warm through.

2. Spread 1 tablespoon of the butter over the bread, then turn all four slices over so that they are butter side down.

3. Spread the mayonnaise over two of the slices, then layer the pork, ham, chillies, gherkins (pickles) and cheese on top. Spread the mustard on the other two slices of bread and then place on top of the sandwich, mustard side down and butter side up.

4. Add the remaining tablespoon butter to the griddle pan and, once it has melted, carefully lift the sandwiches into the pan. Press them down so that they go golden and crispy. After 6–8 minutes, flip over and press down on the other side for another 6–8 minutes. Serve immediately.

Say cheese!

PRESSING THE SANDWICH WILL MAKE THE SWEET EGGY BREAD GO LOVELY AND CRISPY.

THE PEACHY KEEN
(ROASTED PEACH, RICOTTA, LAVENDER & HONEY ON RYE)

This toastie is inspired by a wonderful breakfast I once had in a sunny cafe in Australia. The creaminess of the ricotta is delicious with the caramelized peach and honey.

2 peaches, ripe but still a little firm,
   stoned and sliced into eighths
4 tablespoons clear honey
2 tablespoons softened butter
4 slices of rye sourdough,
   2cm (¾ in) thick

250g (8 oz) ricotta
a sprig of lavender
zest of ½ lemon
salt and freshly ground black pepper

—————————— SERVES 2 ——————————

1. Place a non-stick frying pan over a medium heat.

2. Lay the peach slices in the pan. After 10 minutes, when they are starting to caramelize, flip them over to cook on the other side for a few minutes more. Drizzle over 2 tablespoons of the honey.

3. Meanwhile, spread the butter on all four slices of bread. Turn two slices over so they are butter side down, and divide the ricotta between them, spreading it evenly. Top with the caramelized peach slices, then sprinkle over the lavender. Top with the other two slices of bread, butter side up so the butter is on the outside of the sandwich.

4. Place the sandwiches in the pan to cook. After 5 minutes, when they are starting to char and look golden, drizzle the remaining honey all over them so that it soaks into the bread to create a lovely, sticky mess. Sprinkle with the lemon zest and a little salt and pepper. Enjoy!

Say cheese!

IF YOU DON'T LIKE
LAVENDER, TRY REPLACING
IT WITH ROSEMARY.

DRIZZLED
WITH
HONEY

CHAPTER TWO

SENSATIONAL SANDWICHES FOR SPECIAL OCCASIONS

TOWERING CREATIONS OF OOZY CHEESY EXTRAVAGANCE

THE LEBANESE BREAKFAST
(FLATBREADS WITH MUHAMMARA, EGGS, AVOCADO & CHEESE)

Muhammara is a spicy Lebanese dip made with red peppers and walnuts.
It goes brilliantly with eggs, so this makes a great brunch.

2 Lebanese flat breads
100g (4 oz) Cheddar, grated
1 tablespoon olive oil
2 eggs
1 avocado, peeled, stoned and sliced
6 cherry tomatoes, sliced
salt and freshly ground black pepper
Quick Pickled Onions (see page 34),
dried chilli flakes and freshly chopped
  coriander, to serve

FOR THE MUHAMMARA

150g (1 ½ cups) walnuts
50g (⅓ cup) almonds
100g (½ cup) jarred roasted red (bell)
  peppers, drained
50g (¼ cup) harissa
2 tablespoons pomegranate molasses
½ tablespoon ground cumin
50ml (¼ cup) olive oil
½ teaspoon dried chilli flakes
juice of ½ lemon

SERVES 2

1. Begin by making the muhammara.
   Place a dry frying pan over a low
   heat. Add the walnuts and almonds
   and toast for 5 minutes until golden.
   Set aside to cool.

2. Once they are cool, add the nuts to a
   food processor, along with the (bell)
   peppers, harissa, molasses, cumin,
   olive oil, chilli flakes and lemon juice.
   Blend to a paste.

3. When you are ready to cook, preheat
   the grill (broiler) to high. Unroll the
   flatbreads and place them on a
   roasting tray. Generously spread
   with muhammara, then top with the

cheese. Place under the grill (broiler)
for about 5 minutes until the cheese
is bubbling.

4. Meanwhile, heat the oil in a non-stick
   frying pan over a medium–high heat
   and fry the eggs to your liking.

5. Remove the flatbreads from the grill
   (broiler) and place a fried egg on
   each one. Arrange the sliced avocado
   and tomatoes around the eggs, then
   season with salt and pepper and
   scatter over the chilli flakes.
   Sprinkle with coriander and
   quick-pickled onions
   and serve.

THE NEW YORKER
(GRILLED CHEESE REUBEN WITH SAUERKRAUT & RUSSIAN DRESSING)

There are conflicting claims as to where the classic Reuben sandwich was invented, but it's often associated with New York. Here's my version.

4 slices of sourdough, 2cm (¾ in) thick
2 tablespoons softened butter
180g (6 oz) salt beef, sliced
6 gherkins (pickles), halved lengthways
50g (½ cup) sauerkraut
1 teaspoon chopped fresh dill
6 slices Swiss cheese (Emmental or raclette)

FOR THE DRESSING

4 tablespoons mayonnaise
2 tablespoons tomato ketchup
   (for my smoky version, see page 8)
1 teaspoon Worcestershire sauce
½ tablespoon horseradish sauce
1 tablespoon chopped fresh dill
1 banana shallot, finely diced

— SERVES 2 —

1. To make the dressing, mix all the dressing ingredients together in a small bowl or jar and set aside.

2. Butter the sourdough slices, then turn them over and spread half of the dressing over the other side of all four slices. Reserve the rest of the dressing to serve.

3. Place a frying pan over a medium heat to warm up while you get building.

4. Build your sandwiches in this order: pickles, sauerkraut, cheese, salt beef, more cheese, then dill. Top with the other slices of bread, butter side out, and very carefully place the sandwiches in the pan.

5. After 8–10 minutes, when they are starting to go golden and gooey, carefully turn the sandwiches over to cook on the other side. You might prefer to transfer them to the oven at 180°C/350°F/gas mark 4 to finish melting – this recipe makes for quite a tower!

6. Serve with the remaining Russian dressing on the side.

THE HIPSTER
(WHIPPED GOATS' CHEESE, ROASTED SQUASH & KALE)

Best enjoyed whilst sporting a beard and riding a fixed gear bike.

½ butternut squash, peeled
1 tablespoon olive oil
½ teaspoon dried chilli flakes
½ teaspoon ground nutmeg
½ teaspoon paprika
handful of baby kale, torn and stalks
   removed

juice of 1 lemon
2 tablespoons softened butter
4 slices of seeded rye bread,
   2cm (¾ in) thick
125g (4 ½ oz) soft goats' cheese
salt and freshly ground black pepper

SERVES 2

1. Preheat the oven to 180°C/350°F/gas mark 4.

2. Finely slice the squash – aim for slices about 1cm (½ in) thick. Thin slices will caramelize and cook quickly.

3. Use your hands to the rub the oil and spices all over the squash slices, and give a good sprinkling of salt and pepper. Place in the oven and roast for 15 minutes until soft, sticky and golden, turning several times.

4. Meanwhile, place the kale in a bowl and stir through the lemon juice. This will help to soften it slightly.

5. Butter the bread, then turn the slices over. Layer the goats' cheese, kale and squash on two of the slices of bread. Top with the other slices, butter-side up, and press down.

6. Place a non-stick frying pan over a medium–high heat and carefully lift the sandwiches into the pan. Cook for 5 minutes on each side until golden brown. The cheese can get very runny if overcooked; if it's getting too messy to melt it in the pan, you can pop it in the oven at 180°C/350°F/gas mark 4 for 8–10 minutes instead.

THE POSH ONE
(WHOLE CAMEMBERT FOCACCIA)

Who says you can't have a cheese toastie at a dinner party? This is the ultimate sharing cheesy dish for when you're feeling a little fancy. It takes a little longer than the rest, and you'll need an oven, but it's so worth it.

1 250g (8 oz) Camembert wheel
1 round focaccia (about 400g/1 lb)
3 garlic cloves, peeled and halved

2 sprigs of rosemary, chopped
olive oil, for drizzling
sea salt

SERVES 4

1. Preheat the oven to 180°C/ 350°F/ gas mark 4.

2. Using a knife, carefully slice the top off the round focaccia. Now cut a circle about the same size as the Camembert into the bread, carefully hollowing it out – but make sure you don't cut all the way through. Place the cheese wheel inside the bread. Transfer it to a baking tray.

3. Make a series of slits in the top of the cheese and poke the pieces of garlic into these slits. Do the same with the pieces of rosemary, then

drizzle with oil and sprinkle over some salt. Place the 'lid' of the bread back on top and pop into the oven for 15–20 minutes.

4. Once it's done, remove from the oven and let it cool for about 5 minutes before taking it to the table so that everyone can dig in with torn bread and spoons.

THE MAC & CHEESE CARB FEST

You know what's even better than carbs and cheese?
More carbs and more cheese. This is the lovechild of mac and cheese
and the toastie. Why choose one when you can have both?

FOR THE MAC & CHEESE

250g (9 oz) macaroni
60g (¼ cup) plain flour
1 teaspoon mustard powder
1 teaspoon cayenne pepper
500ml (2 cups) milk
35g (3 tbsp) butter, plus extra for
    spreading

100g (7 oz) Cheddar, grated
100g (4 oz) Gruyère, grated
100g (7 oz) Lincolnshire Poacher, grated
salt

FOR THE BUILD

4 slices of sourdough, 2cm (¾ in) thick
sliced jalapeños, to serve (optional)

--- SERVES 2 ---

1. Bring a pan of salted water to the boil over a medium heat. Add the macaroni and cook for 10 minutes, until al dente.

2. Meanwhile, place the flour, mustard powder and cayenne pepper in a bowl and mix together. Slowly add the milk, stirring after each addition.

3. Place a medium saucepan over a low–medium heat and add the butter. Once it has melted, slowly pour in the flour-and-milk mixture, stirring continually to avoid any lumps forming. Add the cheeses and stir again.

4. When the pasta is cooked, drain it and then add it to the pan with the cheese sauce and stir. Scatter in the jalapeños, if using, and stir again.

5. Set a non-stick frying pan over a medium heat. Butter each slice of sourdough bread. Place two of the slices in the frying pan, butter side down. Carefully top each piece with the macaroni and cheese mixture – this bit can get messy, so try not to get it all over the pan. Top each with the remaining slices of bread, this time butter side up. Cook for 6–8 minutes until golden brown, then carefully flip them over and cook for a further 6–8 minutes to brown the other side. Serve and eat immediately.

CARBS

MORE
CARBS

CHEESE

CHEEKY
JALAPENO

THE BIG BLUE
(GORGONZOLA, FIG, HONEY-COATED SEEDS & ROCKET)

This is a very grown-up toastie, with big flavours. The Gorgonzola is rich and creamy and almost sweet. The freshness of the figs cuts through it perfectly, and the honey-coated seeds add a pleasing crunch.

2 tablespoons mixed seeds, such as sunflower and pumpkin
2 tablespoons clear honey, plus extra for drizzling
½ teaspoon dried chilli flakes
grated zest of 1 lemon

2 tablespoons softened butter
4 slices American-style pumpernickel bread
handful of rocket (arugula) leaves
60–100g (2 oz) Gorgonzola dolce
4 firm figs, sliced

SERVES 2

1. Place a dry non-stick frying pan over a low heat. Add the seeds and toast for 2 minutes. Add the honey, lemon zest and chilli flakes and mix well. When the mixture starts to caramelize, scrape onto baking paper and set aside to cool.

2. Butter one side of each slice of bread and place a clean non-stick frying pan over a medium heat to warm up.

3. Turn the bread over so that it is butter-side down, and divide the rocket (arugula) between two of the slices. Crumble over half of the Gorgonzola, followed by the figs (save a couple of slices for garnish). Sprinkle the seed mixture over the top, then the rest of the Gorgonzola. Place the remaining slices of bread on top, butter-side up.

4. Lift the sandwiches carefully into the pan and cook for 4–8 minutes on each side until golden brown. Serve, drizzled with more honey extra fig slices.

THE SOUTHERN FRIED WAFFLE WONDER
(FRIED BUTTERMILK CHICKEN & WAFFLE GRILLED CHEESE)

This makes the ultimate late night snack – a decadent mixture of
sweet waffle, fried chicken and oozy cheese... pure filth. I've given
instructions for making your own waffles, for which you'll need
a waffle maker, but if you prefer you can buy ready-made waffles
instead. This may seem like a lot of effort to go to for
a sandwich, but just you wait. It's totally worth it.

FOR THE FRIED CHICKEN

1 chicken breast, sliced into 1cm (½ in) strips
50ml (¼ cup) buttermilk
juice of 1 lemon
1 teaspoon paprika
500ml (2 cups) cooking oil
100g (½ cup) cornflour (corn starch)
salt and freshly ground black pepper

FOR THE WAFFLES – MAKES 4

250g (1½ cups) plain flour
1½ teaspoons baking powder
1 teaspoon bicarbonate of (baking) soda
pinch of salt
2 eggs, separated
300ml (1¼ cups) milk
1 tablespoon vegetable oil

FOR THE BUILD

1 avocado, peeled, stoned and sliced
4 slices of Cheddar
sriracha mayonnaise, to serve

— SERVES 2 —

1. Preheat the oven to 180°C/350°F/gas
   mark 4.

2. Place the chicken slices in a bowl and
   cover with the buttermilk and lemon
   juice. Stir in the paprika and leave the
   chicken to marinate while you make
   the waffles.

3. For the waffles, place the flour, baking
   powder, bicarbonate of (baking) soda
   and salt in a bowl.

4. In another bowl, whisk together the
   egg yolks, milk and vegetable oil.
   Slowly add this to the flour mixture,
   stirring after each addition.

CONTINUED OVERLEAF

THE SOUTHERN FRIED WAFFLE WONDER (CONT.)

5. In a third bowl, whisk the egg whites until they have soft, fluffy peaks. Carefully fold into the main mixture.

6. Heat up your waffle machine, add the batter and cook the waffles, in batches, according to the machine instructions. Set aside.

7. To cook the chicken, put the cooking oil in a large saucepan over a medium–high heat to heat up. Tip the cornflour (corn starch) onto a plate and season with salt and pepper. Coat each piece of chicken in the flour, making sure it is coated all over. Using a slotted spoon, carefully lower each piece of coated chicken into the hot oil and cook for 4 minutes until golden and cooked through. Set aside to drain on kitchen paper.

8. Now for the fun part – the build! Pile the avocado, fried chicken and cheese onto the waffles, and place into the oven to warm through. Serve drizzled with sriracha mayonnaise and eat immediately!

Say cheese!

IF YOU WANT TO TAKE A REAL SHORTCUT, TRY MAKING THIS WITH PREMADE WAFFLES AND ALREADY FRIED CHICKEN.

THE SUGAR SHACK STACK
(CHEDDAR, MAPLE & BACON PANCAKE TOWER)

These homemade mini pancakes are really easy, but if you're feeling lazy you can buy the readymade packaged ones. Adding cheese to the classic breakfast of maple, bacon and pancakes is a tasty stroke of melty genius that also just happens to help hold the tower together.

— SERVES 2 —

6 rashers (slices) smoked streaky bacon
2 tablespoons good-quality maple
    syrup, plus extra to serve
1 tablespoon olive oil
100g (4 oz) mature Cheddar (such
    as Westcombe), sliced

FOR THE PANCAKES
225g (1 cup) plain flour
½ teaspoon salt
1 teaspoon caster (fine) sugar
1 teaspoon baking powder
50ml (¼ cup) milk
280ml (1 cup, plus 2 tbsp) buttermilk
2 eggs

1. Start by making the pancakes. Sift the flour, salt, sugar and baking powder into a large bowl. In a separate bowl, beat together the milk, buttermilk and eggs. Slowly add this to the flour mixture, whisking gently. Once it is all incorporated, set aside for 30 minutes. You should end up with quite a thick mixture. A few lumps are fine – they will come out when cooking.

2. Preheat the oven to 180°C/350°F/gas mark 4.

CONTINUED OVERLEAF

GENEROUS DRIZZLE
OF MAPLE SYRUP

DELICIOUS CRISPY
BACON

SUGAR SHACK STACK (CONT.)

3. Place a non-stick frying pan over a medium heat and add the bacon. Fry for 6 minutes on each side until it's nice and crispy. Drizzle over a little maple syrup at the end so it goes pleasantly sticky, then remove the bacon from the pan and set aside. Wipe out the pan with kitchen paper.

4. Return the pan to the heat and add the oil. Add 2 tablespoons of batter to the pan to form each pancake. You are aiming for circles 8–10cm (3-4 in) in diameter, and you should be able to fit 2 or 3 in the pan at a time. When the pancakes are starting to bubble and turn golden on the bottom, flip them over and cook for 5 minutes on the other side. Once they are cooked and nicely golden, remove from the pan and keep them warm, wrapped in foil, while you cook the remaining batter. This should make 6–8 pancakes.

5. Now it's time for the build. On an oven tray, layer the pancakes with slices of cheese and bacon into a delicious (and probably somewhat precarious) tower. Carefully transfer to the oven and cook for 10 minutes until the cheese is fully melted.

6. Remove from the oven and serve drizzled with maple syrup.

Say cheese!

IF YOU WANT TO GO ALL OUT, ADD SOME SCRAMBLED EGGS ON THE SIDE. YUM!

BANOFFEE FRENCH TOAST

This is deserving of the honour of being called a grilled cheese sandwich due to the mascarpone layer. It's wonderfully indulgent.

FOR THE PRALINE

4 tablespoons caster (fine) sugar
10g (1tbsp) hazelnuts, chopped

FOR THE CARAMEL DULCE DE LECHE

400g (14 oz) can condensed milk

FOR THE BUILD

4 slices brioche
2 tablespoons mascarpone
2 bananas, halved lengthways
1 egg, whisked with 2 tablespoons milk

SERVES 2

1. Fill a large saucepan with water and boil the can of condensed milk for 2 hours, making sure it is always immersed. Remove and set aside to cool. This will be your dulce de leche.

2. Place a non-stick frying pan over a high heat and melt 3 tablespoons of the sugar with 1 tablespoon water until it turns to caramel. Add the nuts, stir to coat and then pour out onto greaseproof paper. Let cool, then roughly chop.

3. Lay out the slices of brioche. Spread two of them with 1 tablespoon each of dulce de leche and the other two with 1 tablespoon each of mascarpone.

4. Preheat the grill (broiler) to medium. Sprinkle the remaining sugar over the banana slices and briefly grill (broil) to caramelize. Once this is done, place on top of the mascarpone slices and top with the dulce de leche slices to form your sandwiches. Place the sandwiches into the egg mixture and coat both sides, then place in the frying pan over a medium heat. When it starts to go golden, gently turn over. Cut in half and place on serving plates with extra dulce de leche poured over, and a sprinkle of praline.

THE LEANING TOWER OF DOUGHNUTS

Once again, mascarpone saves the day by allowing us to twist the rules of the grilled cheese sandwich to make something sweet. Honestly, this is just like your average grilled cheese sandwich. Except the bread has been replaced with a towering stack of doughnuts. And the cheese is mascarpone. And it's covered with strawberries, cream and chocolate. See, exactly the same...

4 sugared ring doughnuts, sliced in half horizontally (like bagels)
1 tablespoon softened butter
4 tablespoons chocolate and hazelnut spread
4 tablespoons mascarpone

10 strawberries, halved
100ml (½ cup) double (heavy) cream
80g (3 oz) 70% dark chocolate, broken into pieces
½ teaspoon ground cinnamon

SERVES 2

1. Spread the outsides of the doughnuts with butter. On the insides, spread one half of each doughnut with chocolate and hazelnut spread and the other half with mascarpone. Arrange the sliced strawberries in a ring on top of the mascarpone on each slice – you won't need all of the strawberries for this, so set the rest aside. Then top each mascarpone-and-strawberry slice with a chocolate-and-hazelnut-spread slice, making sure the buttered sides are on the outside.

2. Place the chocolate pieces into a heatproof bowl. Place the cream in a small saucepan over a medium–low heat. Once it has warmed through, pour the cream onto the chocolate and slowly stir until the chocolate has melted into the cream. Set aside.

3. Place a non-stick frying pan over a medium heat. Once it's warmed up, carefully place the doughnut sandwiches in the pan. Cook for 2–3 minutes until the sugar on the outside of the doughnuts starts to caramelize. Very carefully flip the doughnut sandwiches to cook on the other side for 2–3 minutes.

4. Once they are beautifully golden and caramelized, transfer to a serving plate. Stack them carefully and surround with the remaining strawberries. Drizzle generously with the chocolate sauce, sprinkle with cinnamon and serve.

DRIZZLES OF
MELTY CHOCOLATE

A BIG THANKS TO...

My dream team, Tom and Agathe, for making this happen
so quickly and just being just lush in all ways possible

Rob, my love, for putting up with my cheese dreams and always
saying 'That's the best sandwich I've ever eaten in my life!'
after everything I make. Even when I'm sure it wasn't.

My lovely Manor crew, for eating all the cheese, especially
Monsieur Francis for late-night ideas and creations.

To the wonderful team at Kyle Books, especially Tara,
who came up with this cheesy creation.

Thanks, dudes – you all rock.

xxx